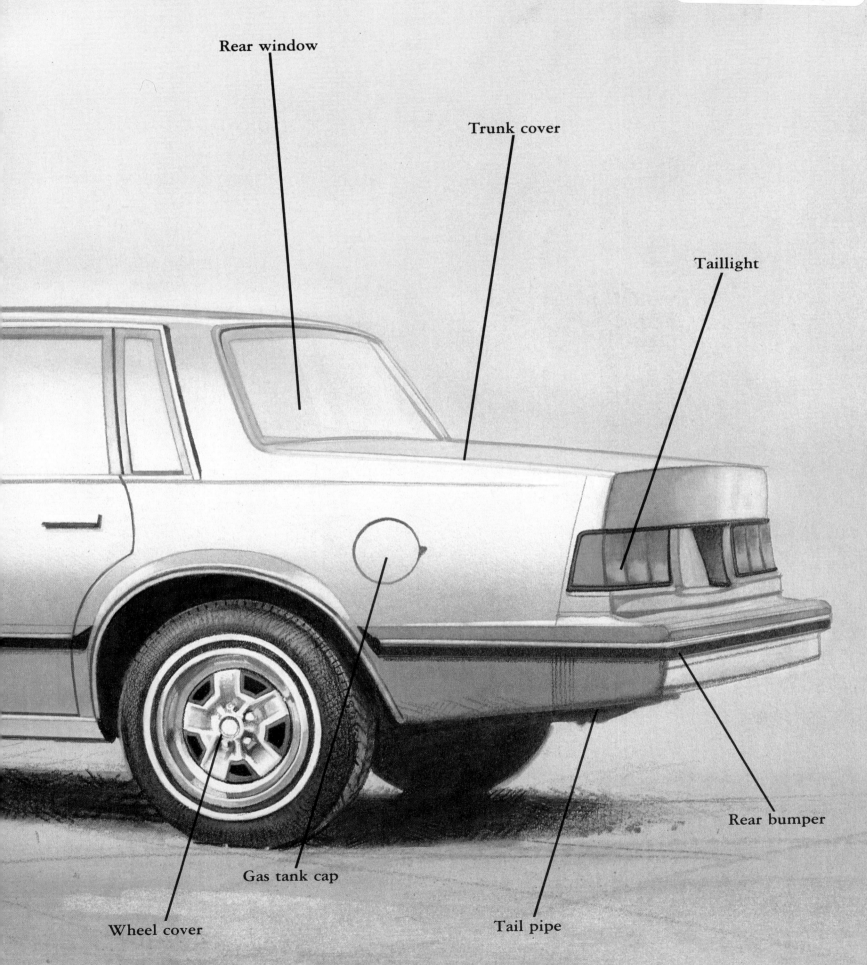

Rear window

Trunk cover

Taillight

Wheel cover

Gas tank cap

Tail pipe

Rear bumper

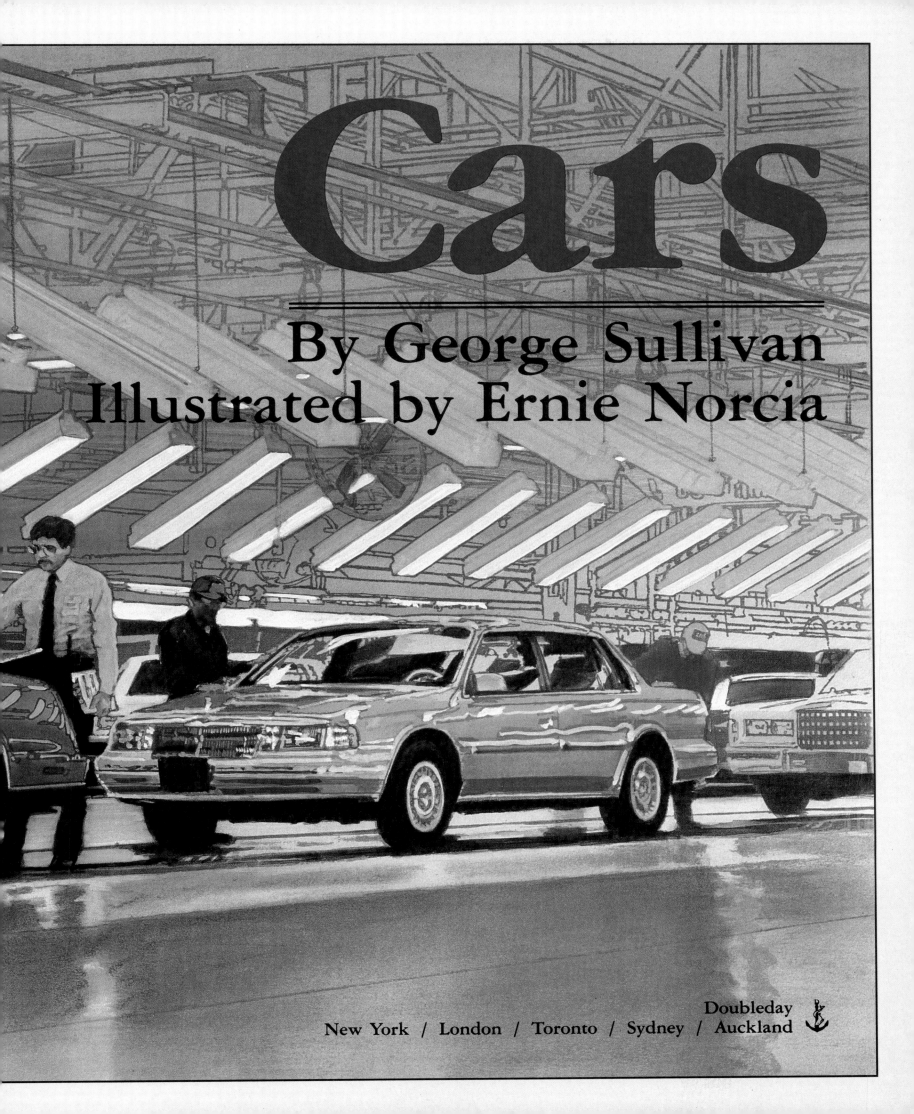

Cars

By George Sullivan
Illustrated by Ernie Norcia

Doubleday

New York / London / Toronto / Sydney / Auckland

Special thanks to Al Rothenberg and Jim
Wren of the Motor Vehicles Manufacturers
Association of the United States, Inc., for
their careful review of the manuscript and
illustrations for this book.
    We also wish to thank Ford Motor
Company for extending invaluable
cooperation to both the author and
illustrator.

Published by Doubleday
a division of Bantam Doubleday Dell
Publishing Group, Inc.,
666 Fifth Avenue, New York, NY 10103
Doubleday and the portrayal of an anchor
with a dolphin are trademarks of
Doubleday, a division of Bantam
Doubleday Dell Publishing Group, Inc.
Library of Congress Cataloging-in-
Publication Data
Sullivan, George, 1927–
    Cars / by George Sullivan ; illustrated
by Ernie Norcia. — 1st ed.
        p.   cm.
    Includes index.
    Summary: Explains how a car is made,
discussing modern production techniques
and following the process from research
and design to manufacturing and
assembly.
    1. Automobiles—Juvenile literature.
[1. Automobiles—Design and
construction.] I. Norcia, Ernie, ill.
II. Title.
TL147.S85   1991
629.2'3—dc19   89-1577   CIP   AC
ISBN 0-385-26068-7
ISBN 0-385-26069-5 (lib. bdg.)
RL: 3.8

Cars! Cars! Cars!

The United States is often called a nation on wheels—and it's no wonder. When Americans want to go from one place to another, they almost always go by car.

Automobiles carry people to work, to shop, and to school. People use their cars to go to the movies or the beach. They use them when they want to play tennis or golf or go boating. They use them to visit distant vacation spots, where they can fish, hike, or ski.

Millions of jobs depend on cars. People design cars and build them. People work in the steel, glass, rubber, and plastic industries, to provide materials to make cars. Other people sell gas, oil, and tires and fix cars.

Before people had automobiles, they walked or rode bicycles when traveling short distances. They also rode horses and used trolley cars and horse-drawn wagons or carriages. In fact, the first automobiles were sometimes called "horseless carriages."

In the early days of the automobile, only the very rich could afford them. But during the 1920s and 1930s, as the giant automobile industry developed, more and more people were able to buy them. Today, about nine out of ten American families own at least one car. Half of all families own two or more cars.

By the year 2000, more than 500 million cars will have been built, most of them in the United States.

Some people say we are living in the space age. Others say it's the computer age. But cars affect our lives more than any other product. Year in, year out, we live in the age of the automobile.

The Team

Some new cars are fresh creations. Others are simply improved versions of existing models. In either case, before a new car begins to take shape, a team is formed to work on it. The team is made up of many hundreds of people. Some of these people decide what the car is going to look like. Others plan how powerful the engine will be. Still others decide where and how the car will be manufactured. Salespeople make plans to promote and market the car.

Members of the team trade ideas and opinions. Their goal: to build a car that has good looks, gives a good ride, is safe, and will have a long life—and build it at the least possible cost.

Planning a new car also begins with the people who are going to buy it—the customers. Experts in market research send interviewers to every part of the country to get opinions and suggestions from car owners. The planning department wants to find out what kind of car the average motorist would like to own. What color and size? How powerful should the engine be? What accessories should be included?

An interviewer may knock at the door of your home one day and say: "I'm working on a study of automobile owners. Would you please answer a few questions for me?"

Then the interviewer might ask:

"What would you rather have in your next car—greater fuel economy or a more powerful engine?"

"What would be more important—more space in the trunk or more legroom in the backseat?"

Several other questions might concern accessories:

"Do you want your new car to have special lightweight wheels and racing-style tires?" the interviewer might ask. "What about an AM/FM stereo radio/cassette or CD [compact disk] player?"

The interviews with car owners provide only part of the information that is important to the planning team. Perhaps there has been a technological development that enables the engine to burn less gasoline. The efficient use of fuel is always important. This development will be included in the new model.

One problem with automobiles is the fumes that are given off by the engine exhaust. These fumes pollute the air. The United States Government requires automakers to equip cars with antipollution devices. The planning team is sure to provide for such a device on the new model.

On the basis of the information it gets, the planning team decides what size the new car should be—how wide, how long, how high. The team decides what kind of engine it should have. They recommend certain accessories. They report on how much it will cost to build the car and how much the company should charge for it. Once the plans have been approved, stylists and engineers begin designing the car.

It often takes three or four years to design, develop, and test a new car. Manufacturing and assembly plants have to be designed for it. Then production begins.

Designing the New Model

O nce plans for the new model have been completed, designers prepare sketches by the hundreds. The sketches show what the new model is going to look like, inside and out.

From the sketches, a full-sized model of the car is made out of clay. The model has plastic windows and plastic molding strips. The tires and wheels, the headlights and taillights, are the real thing, however. Once the clay model has been given a glossy finish, it looks exactly like what the steel-bodied car is going to look like.

Meanwhile, another design team is building a full-sized plywood model of the car's interior, including the seats and instrument panel. From the model, the designers will be able to learn whether the interior is roomy enough. Can the driver and passengers get in and out of the car with ease? Are the instrument controls easy to get at?

Actual paints and fabrics are used in the model. Decisions concerning colors must be made. Each model may have as many as five or six color variations. But colors must match the car's image. Bright red is for sporty models. Dark colors usually go with big luxury cars.

Wind-Tunnel Testing

Once the clay model has been built, it undergoes a series of wind-tunnel tests. A wind tunnel is shaped like a huge cylinder. An enormous fan blade is mounted at one end of the tunnel. The fan blade weighs more than a ton. It can send air blasting through the tunnel at hurricane speed.

Engineers who do wind-tunnel tests are concerned about *drag.* Drag is the air that pushes against a moving car, holding it back. When the outside of the car is smooth and rounded, little drag is created. The air slips right by. The car is easier to handle and uses less fuel. But a car with a boxy body may have too much drag. The wind-tunnel tests may show the car's shape has to be changed.

Once the clay model is in place in the tunnel and the huge fan whirring, an engineer stands in front of the car. The engineer holds a hollow metal tube with an L-shaped bend at one end. When the engineer presses a lever near the handle, a thin plume of smoke bursts from the tube's end. The trail of smoke quickly travels the length of the car.

As air is sent through the tunnel at different speeds, engineers watch the plume of smoke. The smoke enables them to see the air-flow pattern. It is easy for them to spot areas where drag may be a problem. The wind-tunnel tests may show that the car's front end is too high or that the front windshield has to be tilted a little bit more. These changes will be included in the car's final design.

Designing for Safety

Automobiles and their wide use have caused some serious problems. Auto accidents are one problem. About forty-five thousand people are killed in accidents in the United States each year. Another 3 million people are injured.

Automakers never stop trying to design and build safer cars. They have two safety goals. One is to help the driver avoid accidents.

The self-adjusting mirror is a recent advance in the field of safety. At night, when headlights are shining behind the car, a photosensor mounted above the mirror senses the headlights and automatically dims their reflection. When no headlights are shining, the mirror automatically switches back to normal.

Designers and engineers are also concerned about preventing injuries should an accident take place. This is how airbags help. Stored in the steering wheel and in a panel facing the front seat, airbags prevent front-seat passengers from being pitched forward. Beginning in the late 1980s, no American car was designed without airbags.

Designers and engineers use life-sized dummies to test cars for safety. In one test, a dummy is placed in a seated position on what is called an *impact sled.* A steering wheel has been mounted in front of the sled's seat.

After safety belts have been placed about the dummy's shoulders and waist, the sled is hauled to the top of a steep ramp, then released. Down the ramp the sled hurtles. When the sled crashes into the barrier, the dummy is thrown forward. Computers and slow-motion cameras record what happens. Such tests help in developing dependable safety belts and safer steering wheels. The deep-dish steering wheel was developed through such tests.

Computer-Aided Design

While stylists and designers are working to make the car look good, engineers are concerned about making it run well. They're drawing up the plans for each of the more than thirteen thousand parts that will go into the car.

In days past, these parts had to be designed by means of hand-drawn sketches, a process that took years. Those days have gone the way of the horse-drawn carriage. Today, engineers rely on the computer.

Once the clay model of the car is completed, an electronic probe locates thousands of points on the model's surface. These points are translated into numbers which are programmed into a computer. The computer changes the numbers into an image of the model, then projects that image on the screen.

As the various individual parts for the new car are designed, each is given a number and programmed into the computer. Each can then be displayed on the computer's screen.

Engineers can make the parts on the screen move just as they will move on the finished car. Windows roll up and down, window wipers wipe, and the steering wheel turns to the left and right. The computer can test the strength of each part and report exactly how much wear it can take.

Different body styles can be tested. More powerful or less powerful engines can be tried out. The drawings on the screen can be pulled apart and made to appear in solid form or three dimensions. Shapes and angles of a part can be changed. Different color combinations can be given a try.

Computers don't design cars or engineer the parts. People do. But computers have speeded up the process. What used to take months, even years, can now be done in hours and days.

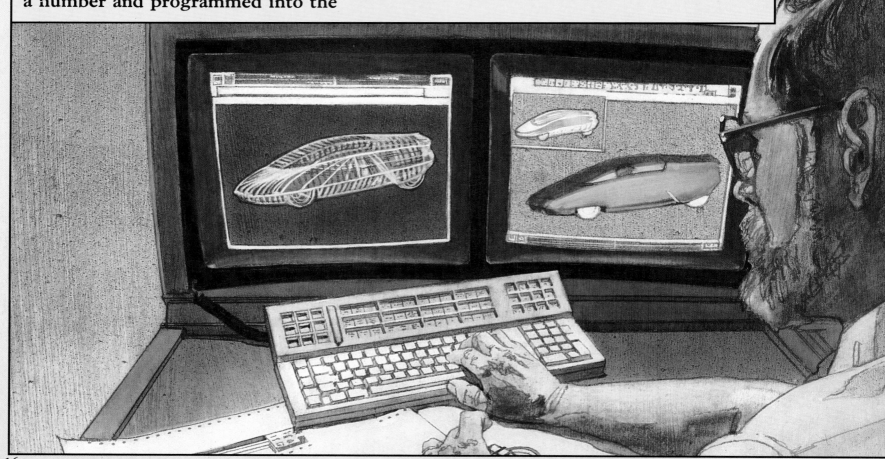

An engineer building a model, or prototype, from a blueprint to make sure that all parts fit properly

Building the Prototypes

The planning department and design team have finished their work. The engineers have designed the car's parts. There is still one question that must be answered, however: Can the manufacturer produce the car at a profit? If the answer is yes, the company builds test models of the car. It may build a dozen or more of them,

each a perfect duplicate of the other. The models are called prototypes.

The prototypes are tested to make sure all of the parts and systems work efficiently. Some tests are done in laboratories. Others are done on highways and on special test tracks called *proving grounds.* The testing goes on twenty-four hours a day, seven days a week, for months.

Testing the Prototypes

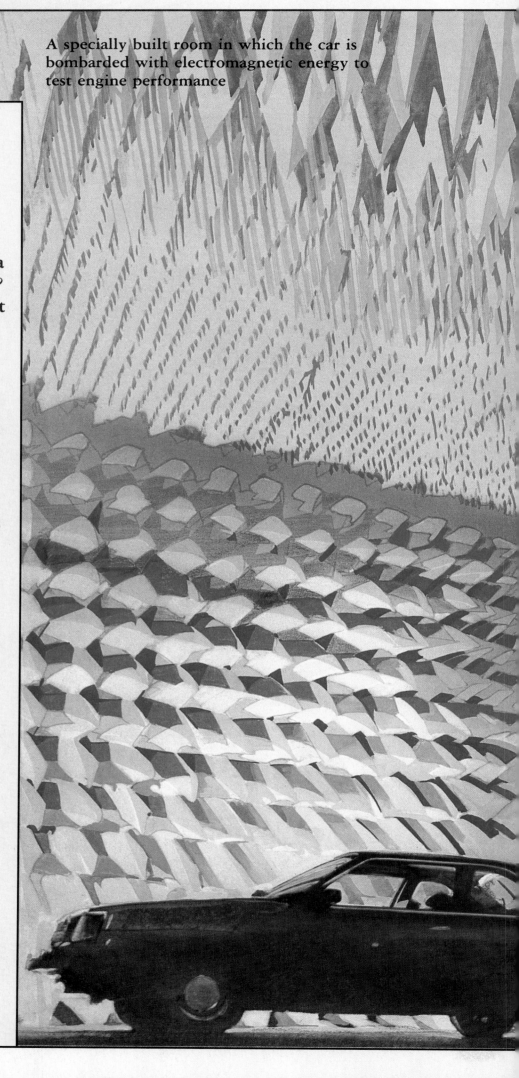

A specially built room in which the car is bombarded with electromagnetic energy to test engine performance

Who wants a car with a windshield that leaks or a radio that goes *"Zzzzz"?* A splash test helps spot leaks. A prototype is put into a sealed room that is just big enough for it. Jets of water blast at the car for several hours. Then the inside of the car is inspected. Are there any wet spots? A windshield that leaks may have to be redesigned.

Computer tests are used to find out whether the radio can cope with electrical interference. The prototype is also driven near high-power transmission lines. If the power lines cause static, the radio needs more electronic shielding.

Special "torture machines" are used to test car parts. Through the tests, the car experiences years of wear and tear in a matter of days or weeks. A mechanical arm opens and closes each door as many as eighty thousand times to be sure that the latches and hinges do not fail. A light switch may be turned on and off as many as half a million times. Windshield wipers have been made to sweep back and forth 3 million times. The horn blares and blares until it fails.

A prototype is taken out onto a special test track. A skilled driver gets behind the wheel. He or she races the car around the track at speeds of up to a hundred miles an hour for fifty-five minutes. When the driver's shift ends,

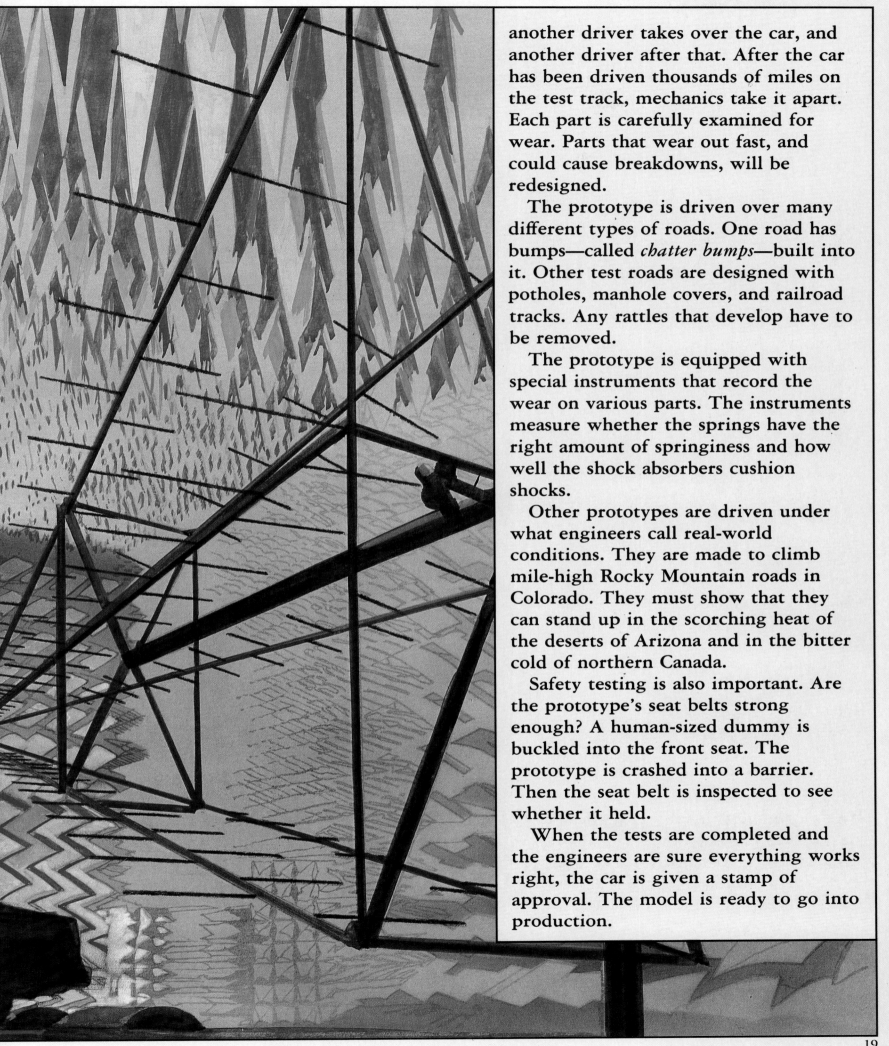

another driver takes over the car, and another driver after that. After the car has been driven thousands of miles on the test track, mechanics take it apart. Each part is carefully examined for wear. Parts that wear out fast, and could cause breakdowns, will be redesigned.

The prototype is driven over many different types of roads. One road has bumps—called *chatter bumps*—built into it. Other test roads are designed with potholes, manhole covers, and railroad tracks. Any rattles that develop have to be removed.

The prototype is equipped with special instruments that record the wear on various parts. The instruments measure whether the springs have the right amount of springiness and how well the shock absorbers cushion shocks.

Other prototypes are driven under what engineers call real-world conditions. They are made to climb mile-high Rocky Mountain roads in Colorado. They must show that they can stand up in the scorching heat of the deserts of Arizona and in the bitter cold of northern Canada.

Safety testing is also important. Are the prototype's seat belts strong enough? A human-sized dummy is buckled into the front seat. The prototype is crashed into a barrier. Then the seat belt is inspected to see whether it held.

When the tests are completed and the engineers are sure everything works right, the car is given a stamp of approval. The model is ready to go into production.

Producing the Parts

Once the green light has been given to manufacture the car, the parts are ordered. A modern automobile is made up of thirteen thousand parts. They are made of materials of every type. Great quantities of steel, aluminum, plastic, rubber, and glass are used. Cotton and synthetic fibers go into the seat covers. Leather may be used on the dashboard. Sugarcane is sometimes used for insulating the roof.

Some metal parts are formed by pouring molten metal into a mold and letting it cool and harden. This type of part is called a casting. The engine block—the core of the engine—is one such casting.

Other parts, such as fenders, doors, side panels, and the roof, are stamped out. Huge, heavy presses, each as tall as a two-story building, crash down on thin sheets of steel, pressing each sheet into the desired shape. Each press works something like a cookie cutter. But the machine is so big and powerful the floor shakes each time it presses out a part. And the noise, says one worker, "is the same as when you throw a Volkswagen off the roof of a twenty-story building." Workers must wear special earplugs to help protect their hearing.

While some parts are made by the car manufacturer, many come from smaller companies called suppliers. Gasoline tanks, batteries, fan belts, and wheel covers are among the thousands of parts that American automakers purchase from the many suppliers throughout the United States.

The Assembly Plant

Imagine a building big enough to hold six or seven football fields side by side, and tall enough to put a two- or three-story building inside. That's what an automobile assembly plant looks like.

Step into the plant and what you notice first is noise. There's the crash and clatter of sheets of steel being fed into huge welding machines. In a welding machine, two parts that touch are brought to the melting point. They flow together. In cooling they become one piece.

There's the rumble of conveyors carrying long lines of completed car bodies from one work station to the next. There's the clang of warning bells from four-wheeled automated stock carriers. Workers must sometimes shout to be heard.

Sparks fly from the tips of welding torches. Four-wheeled electrically powered vehicles, many about the size of golf carts, dart back and forth over the concrete floors. Many tow wheeled racks filled with auto parts. Some people travel about on bicycle.

In this hubbub, workers and robots put together the thirteen thousand parts that make up an automobile. The parts arrive throughout the day and night by truck and train. Inside the plant, there are many acres of storage space where metal racks and bins containing parts are parked.

A group of robots welding the front sections of automobiles as these sections move along on the assembly line

23

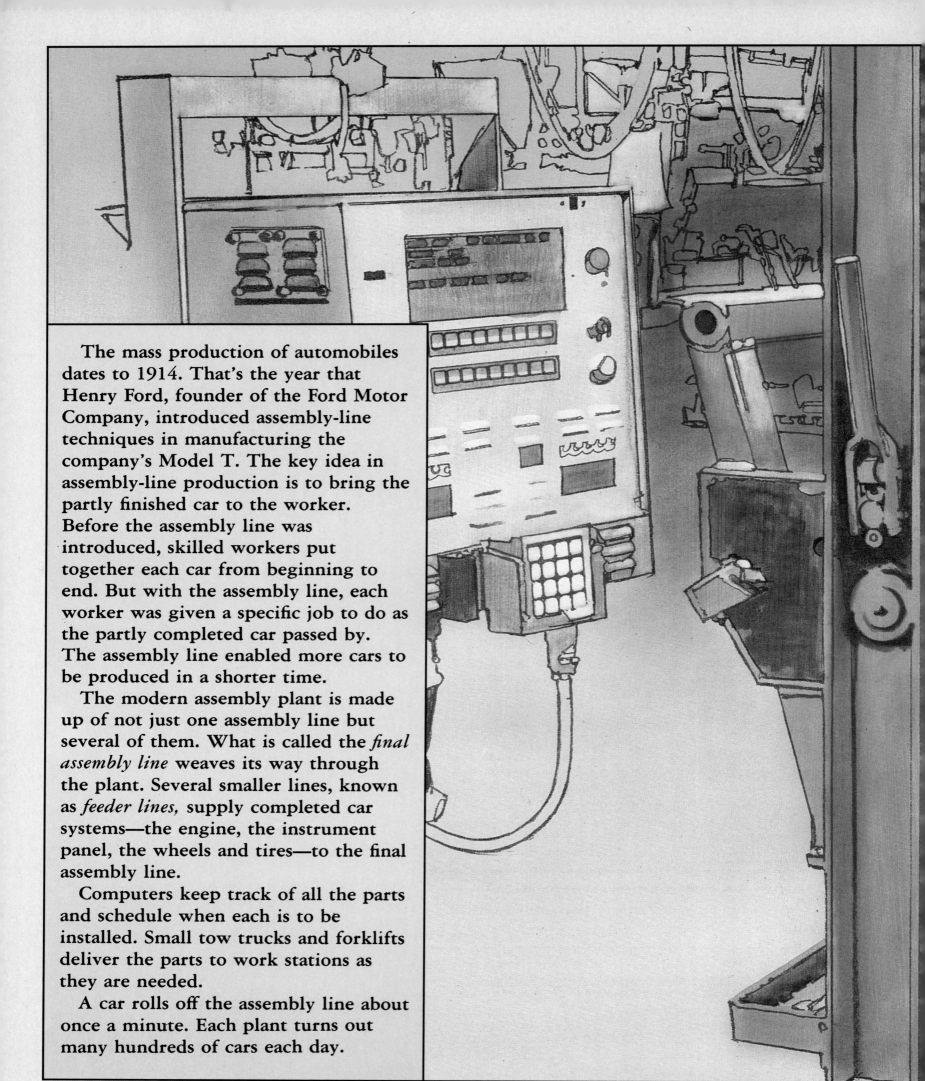

The mass production of automobiles dates to 1914. That's the year that Henry Ford, founder of the Ford Motor Company, introduced assembly-line techniques in manufacturing the company's Model T. The key idea in assembly-line production is to bring the partly finished car to the worker. Before the assembly line was introduced, skilled workers put together each car from beginning to end. But with the assembly line, each worker was given a specific job to do as the partly completed car passed by. The assembly line enabled more cars to be produced in a shorter time.

The modern assembly plant is made up of not just one assembly line but several of them. What is called the *final assembly line* weaves its way through the plant. Several smaller lines, known as *feeder lines,* supply completed car systems—the engine, the instrument panel, the wheels and tires—to the final assembly line.

Computers keep track of all the parts and schedule when each is to be installed. Small tow trucks and forklifts deliver the parts to work stations as they are needed.

A car rolls off the assembly line about once a minute. Each plant turns out many hundreds of cars each day.

People

Visiting a modern automobile plant is something like visiting a factory of the future. Computers are at work everywhere, controlling production and the delivery of parts. Electronic devices are used for inspecting and testing. There are robots of several different types.

But despite the futuristic technology, at the heart of the automobile plant are the men and women who work there. At some plants, there are thousands of them.

Kevin and Maria are two such workers. Each drives to work five mornings a week, parking in the huge plant lot. Each wears a badge with his or her picture. The badge is color-coded to indicate the department in which each works. As Kevin and Maria enter the plant, a computer scans their badges. From that moment on, they are officially at work.

Maria works in the quality-control department. As each car moves down the assembly line, it stops briefly in front of Maria. She checks to see that each car door closes properly and that the gas tank cover fits tightly.

In one hand, Maria holds an electronic keyboard. If she finds something wrong, Maria uses the keyboard to communicate with the work station responsible for the problem. The workers at the work station quickly correct it.

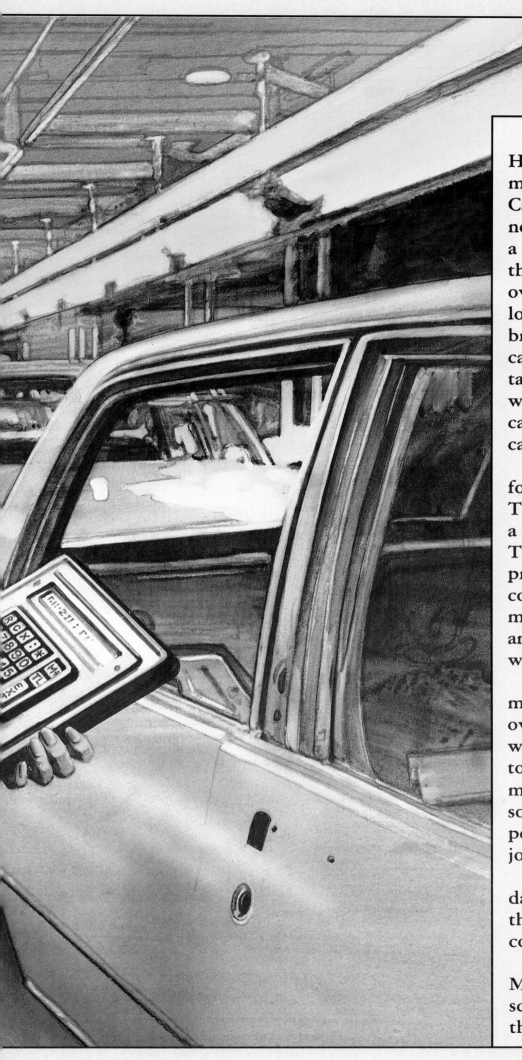

Kevin works in the trim department. He is a carpet installer. One by one, the moving cars stop in front of Kevin. Carpets of different colors are stacked nearby. Moving briskly, Kevin chooses a front-seat carpet of the right color for the car before him. He flips it in place over the car's bare steel floor, carefully looping a precut hole over the hand-brake handle. A coworker grasps the carpet from the other side and pulls it taut. Together, they smooth out any wrinkles. Just as they've finished, the car begins moving again and another car arrives.

Maria belongs to a group of thirty or forty workers within her department. The members meet two or three times a month in one of the plant cafeterias. They discuss how to improve production methods and working conditions. Not long ago, one of the members of Maria's group introduced an idea to prevent seat covers from wrinkling.

Working in an auto plant used to mean doing the same job over and over, and perhaps doing it for years without change. Things are different today. Maria, who is skilled in doing many different jobs, might agree to do someone else's job for a time. Another person in the group will take over her job.

Kevin and Maria work ten hours a day, five days a week. They are given thirty minutes for lunch and several coffee breaks during the day.

When their shift is over, Kevin and Maria leave the plant. The computer scans their badges again and credits them with the hours they have worked.

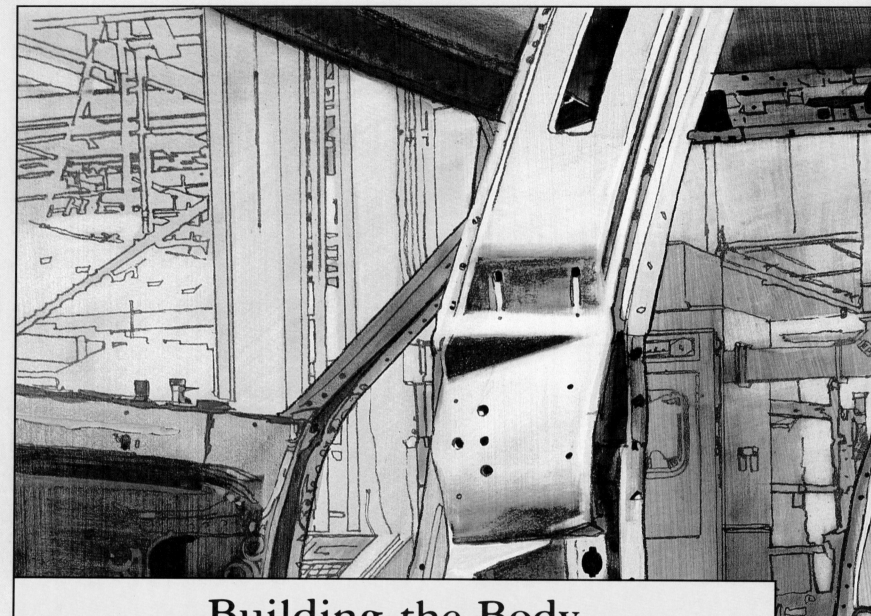

Building the Body

The long process of assembling an automobile begins when a worker grabs a piece of sheet steel off a stock rack and places it upright on the assembly line. Then he or she locks it into place. That piece of steel is one of several that form the car's front end. Special framing fixtures hold the pieces in place while robots weld them together.

As the completed front section moves down the assembly line, the body side panels, the compartment for the trunk, and the roof are added and welded together.

Then the unit is inspected. As it moves along the assembly line, it passes in front of a computer scanner that carefully examines each spot where it has been welded. Any weld not up to standard is reported on the computer screen. A worker watches the screen. He or she reports any defect. Any welding flaw must be corrected.

The body is also checked by a device called an *automatic optical scanner*. This uses laser beams and an electronic camera to make sure that each of the body parts fits properly.

Next, the car's doors, the lid for the trunk, and the hood are added to the body. The next step is to grind smooth all the body surfaces, the final step before the body is painted.

Just in Time

Suppose an assembly plant is scheduled to put together several hundred cars next Thursday, a number of which are four-door, silver-gray sedans with four-cylinder engines and black steering wheels. Then just enough silver-gray doors and other body parts, four-cylinder engines, and black steering wheels must be on hand at the plant that day.

All of the parts arrive just in time to be assembled. When it's the right moment for the four-cylinder engine to be joined to the silver-gray sedan body, the engine arrives at the right place on the assembly line. The worker who is to supervise the installation receives teletyped instructions from the production department. The just-in-time method enables the greatest number of cars to be put together in the shortest possible time.

But the system takes an enormous amount of planning. Once the production department decides on the kinds of cars that are going to be assembled on a particular day, that information is put into a computer. The computer tells the various suppliers what parts are going to be needed that day. The suppliers, in turn, tell the trucking companies and railroads how much space is going to be required to ship the parts. Arrangements are then made for the right number of trailer trucks and freight cars.

A day or so before the Thursday on which the four-door, silver-gray sedans with four-cylinder engines and black steering wheels are to be assembled, the parts start arriving at the plant. The trucks and trains make hundreds of deliveries. Workers who specialize in material handling assign the parts to storage areas within the plant.

Early Thursday morning, the parts are delivered throughout the plant by forklifts and tow trucks, arriving at the right place just in time.

Robot Workers

They receive no salary. They never take a day off. They don't even take coffee breaks. Day after day, they do the same job over and over, and they never complain.

They're industrial robots—self-controlled electronic machines that take the place of human workers. In the automobile industry, tens of thousands of industrial robots perform such assembly-line jobs as welding, painting, and inspecting. The work they do is often too hot, too dirty, or too monotonous for human workers.

Industrial robots don't have a human form, as do the robots in science fiction novels or the movies. They come in many different shapes and sizes. Robots that weld usually have a single metal arm with a boxlike shape that slides in and out. Another type of robot has a camera eye that is programmed to sort parts used in the car's ignition systems. It rejects any parts with defects.

"Alice" is the nickname of a 205-

A robot welder

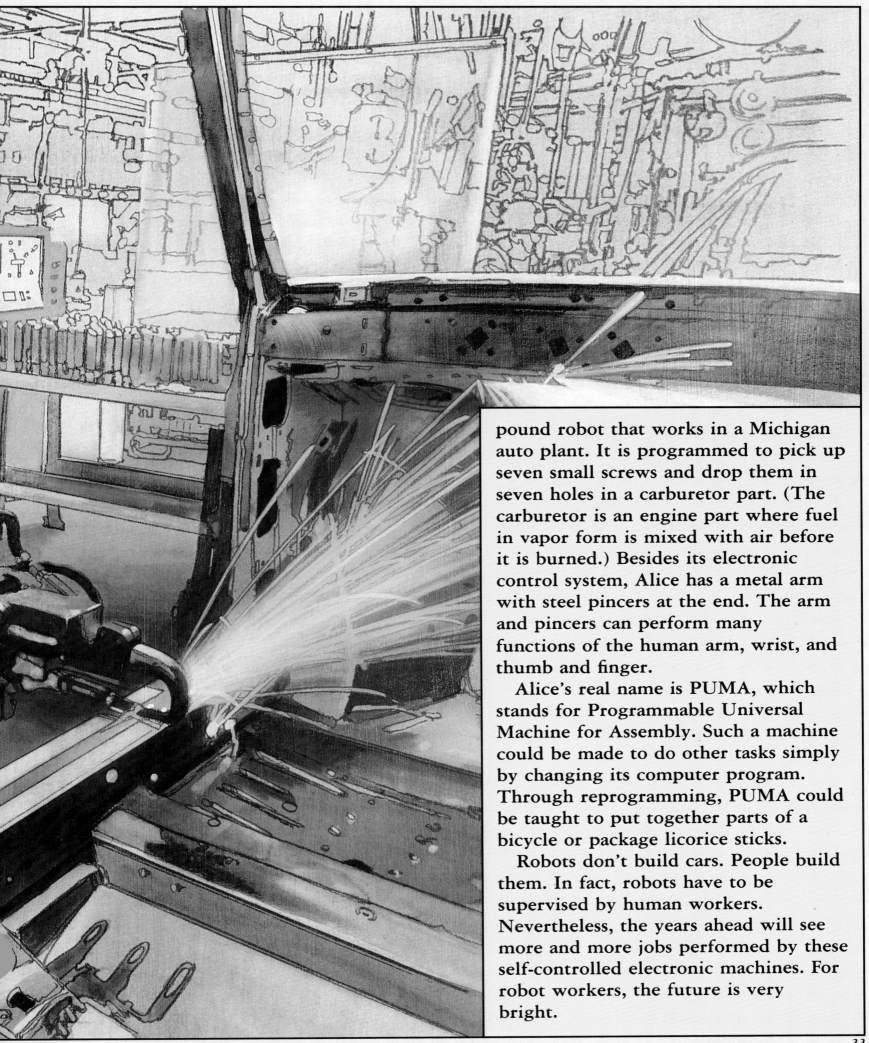

pound robot that works in a Michigan auto plant. It is programmed to pick up seven small screws and drop them in seven holes in a carburetor part. (The carburetor is an engine part where fuel in vapor form is mixed with air before it is burned.) Besides its electronic control system, Alice has a metal arm with steel pincers at the end. The arm and pincers can perform many functions of the human arm, wrist, and thumb and finger.

Alice's real name is PUMA, which stands for Programmable Universal Machine for Assembly. Such a machine could be made to do other tasks simply by changing its computer program. Through reprogramming, PUMA could be taught to put together parts of a bicycle or package licorice sticks.

Robots don't build cars. People build them. In fact, robots have to be supervised by human workers. Nevertheless, the years ahead will see more and more jobs performed by these self-controlled electronic machines. For robot workers, the future is very bright.

Getting Painted

When the overhead conveyor brings the car into the paint department, it is an empty shell of gray steel. When it leaves, it gleams.

The car body not only gets several coats of paint, it gets chemically treated, too. Robot painters do much of the work. Each robot has an arm that can move in many directions. The way the arm moves enables it to spray paint in even the hardest-to-get-at places. Automatic machines are also used to paint the car's body. But the automatic machines can spray paint in only one direction.

First, each car is dipped in a chemical bath to clean it of dust and dirt. Then the joints between the metal sections that form the body are filled with a pastelike substance called *sealer.* Next, the body is dunked in a tank of primer. The primer coat helps to protect the body from rust.

The paint booth, as big as a living room, is the next stop. The air in the paint booth is kept dust-free. The doorway leading into the booth is fitted with an air lock. This sucks the dust out of any air entering the booth. Workers wear dust-resistant coveralls. In addition, there is a film of water on the floor at the booth's entrance. When a worker walks through it, the water rinses any dust from the bottom of the worker's shoes.

The final coats of paint go on inside the paint booth. They are applied *electrostatically.* This means that each tiny droplet of paint is given an electric charge. The drops are then attracted to the metal car body in the same way thumbtacks are attracted to a magnet. As a result, no paint droplets are wasted.

After the car has gotten its final coats of paint, it is sealed with clear enamel. Then the body moves into an oven where the paint is baked to breath-taking brightness. No matter what color the car has become—red, white, black, or blue—it dazzles the eyes.

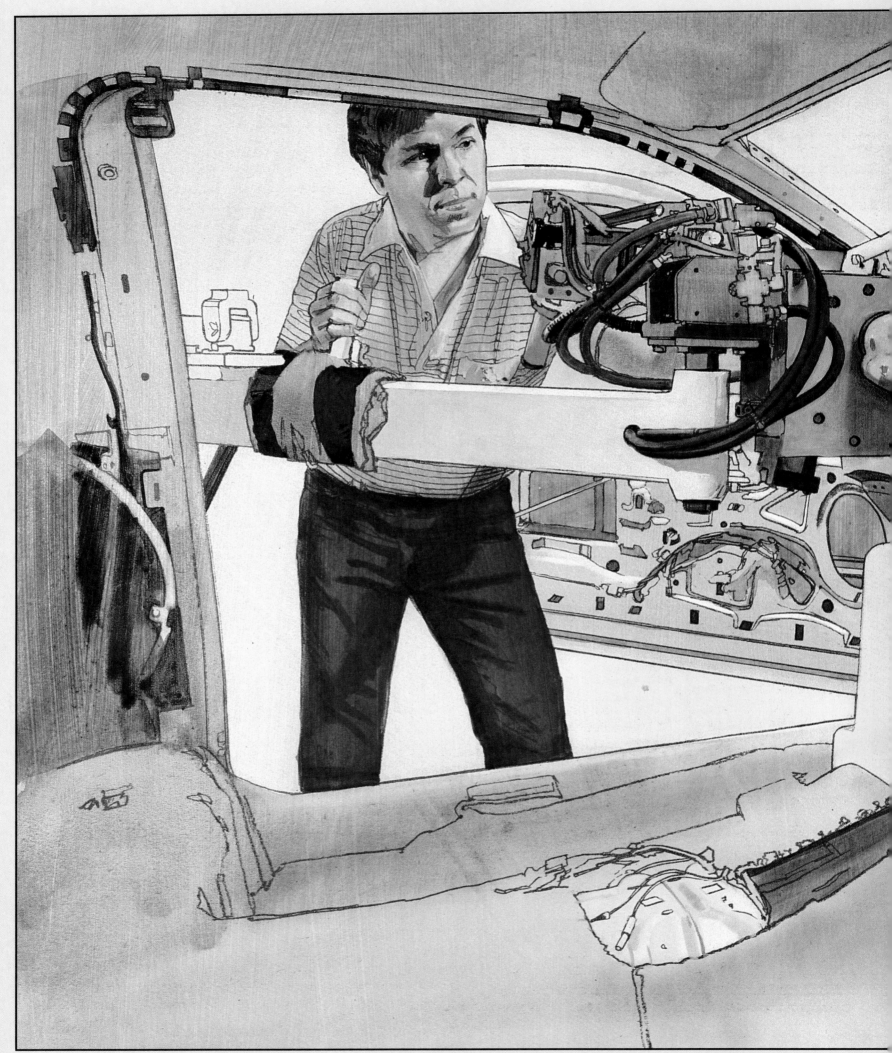

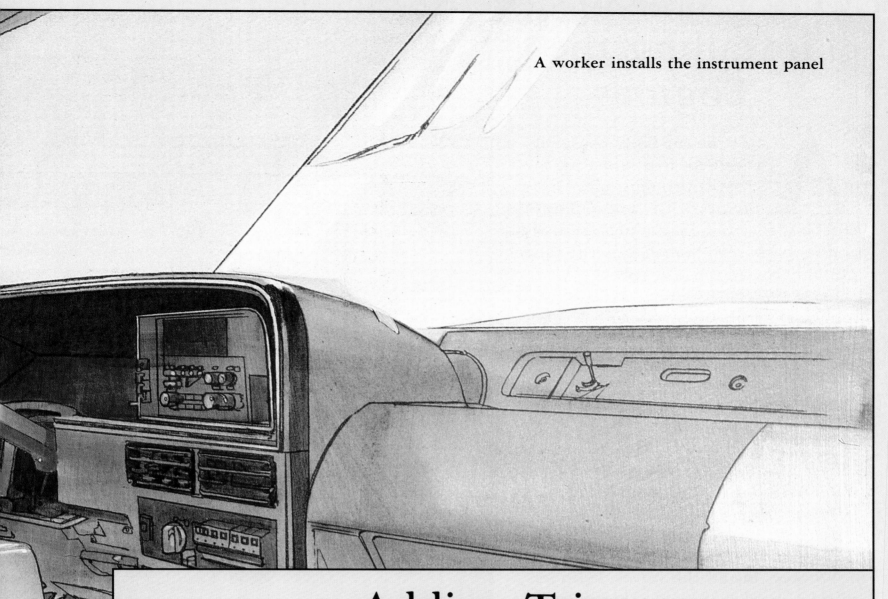

A worker installs the instrument panel

Adding Trim

There are two kinds of trim: hard trim and soft trim. Hard trim includes the instrument panel, steering column, window glass, heater, air conditioner, and electrical wiring. The seats, carpeting, door pads, and ceiling insulation are types of soft trim.

Trim crews work with special care. The wrong move could shatter a piece of glass or damage expensive fabric. At one plant, trim crews installed fifteen thousand windshields without breaking one.

Hard trim is installed first. The instrument panel arrives from its own feeder line. A computer has already matched the instrument panel and style with the right car body. Another feeder line provides the steering column.

Before the instrument panel is locked into place, a member of the trim crew checks each of its systems. Does the radio work properly? What about fuel gauge and trunk release? Is the speedometer accurate? Each system is hooked into a computer. The computer screen must flash "A—OK" for each system. Any item that doesn't get computer approval must be replaced or repaired.

Now the car is beginning to look like a car, not just a pile of car-shaped metal. But it still needs wheels and tires, and there's nothing under the hood.

Installing the Engine

After the car body has been trimmed, it is joined to the chassis (pronounced *chass*-ee, rhymes with classy). The chassis is the frame on which the body and its parts rest. Sometimes it is called the underbody.

Once the chassis and body have been joined, the car's engine is added. The engine has been built on a separate assembly line.

Each engine has its beginning when iron is melted and poured into molds. Each mold forms a heavy engine skeleton, called a *block.* Hundreds of different operations are performed upon each block. It is sanded and polished. Holes, big and small, are bored into it, sometimes from several directions at once.

Workers install the valves, cylinders, pistons, crankshaft, and other parts. This is known as *dressing* the engine. At the end of the line, the transmission is added. The transmission consists of the gears and other parts that transmit the power of the engine to the axle and wheels. Last, the engine is filled with motor oil and other lubricants. It gets an eight-minute test run to check its operation.

Once work on the engine has been completed, it is hoisted onto a ceiling-high conveyor. The car's body, meanwhile, is moving along on a floor-level conveyor. At the right moment, the two lines meet and both are stopped. Then the engine is lowered into the body. Workers tighten bolts with power wrenches to lock the engine in place.

Finishing Touches

After the engine has been installed, workers put down the carpeting in the front and back seats. The bumpers and front grille go on.

The car is still without wheels. On yet another feeder line, a computer is matching the right wheels with the right tires. Then the tires are mounted on the wheels. The wheel-tire assemblies roll down a chute to a point where they can be quickly mounted on the car body.

After the wheels are on, the completed car may get some special striping. To apply a stripe, a worker (known as a *striper)* attaches a metal frame to each side of the car. Then he takes a tube of paint about the size of a large tube of toothpaste. At the end of the tube, there's a small wheel. Using the frame to guide his hand, the striper rolls the wheel along the side of the car. A handsome stripe is the result.

Final Testing

Every car that comes off the assembly line faces a moment of truth. The car is fueled, a worker slips behind the wheel, inserts the key in the ignition, and turns it. The engine roars to life. That sound is a stamp of approval.

Although the parts and systems have been checked at many points along the assembly line, the car must undergo several more tests and inspections. The headlight beams are put in proper adjustment. The wheels get aligned. The brakes get tested. Then the car is given a hard shower. It lasts four minutes. Afterward, all the windows are inspected for leaks.

Each car must also pass a roll test. The car is driven onto two pairs of big steel rollers. The driver presses down on the accelerator, and the car's wheels start turning fast—but the car doesn't go anywhere. That's because the rollers spin as the car's wheels turn. During the roll test, the car's transmission system is checked. If any defective part is spotted, it must be repaired, and then the car is retested. A sign above the final test station declares:

IF IT'S NOT RIGHT,

DON'T SHIP IT.

A roll test

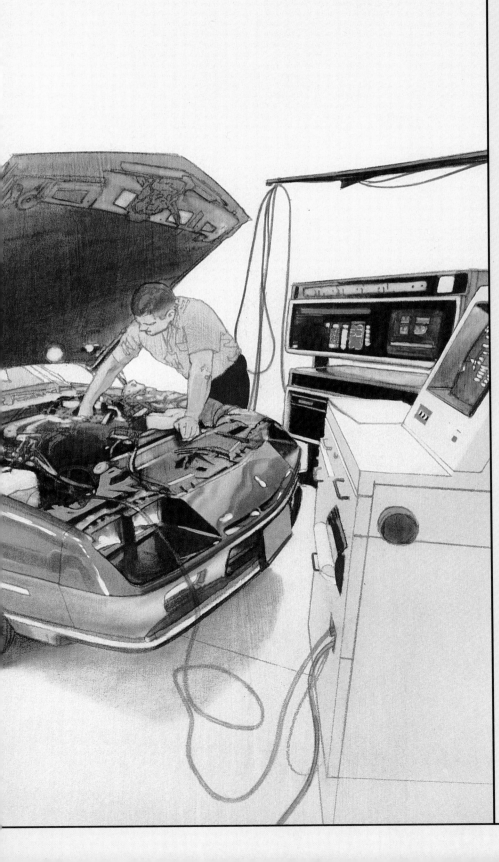

To the Dealer

When the car leaves the assembly plant, it is driven only a few hundred feet to the *convoy yard,* a huge open area as big as a mall parking lot. Cars seldom stay in the convoy yard more than forty-eight hours. They are loaded into trailer trucks and freight cars and sent to the first destination—the automobile dealer. There are new-car dealers throughout the United States, more than twenty-five thousand of them in all.

When the cars arrive at the dealer's showroom, each must be "prepped"—made ready for the customer. The dealer checks the condition of the car's upholstery and seat covers, the sun visor and seat belts. He or she unpacks and inspects the car's tool kit and jack.

All of the car's warning lights, buzzers, and gauges are tested. The headlights, interior lights, and turn signals are checked. Even the tiny light inside the glove compartment is tested.

The dealer uses electronic equipment and computers to test the car's ignition, battery, spark plugs, and other parts of the electrical system. He uses another computer to check the alignment of the wheels. The tires are inspected and the air pressure of each is checked.

Then the car is taken out on the road for a test drive. The brakes and transmission are tested. The heater and the air conditioner and the various instruments on the instrument panel are test-operated. Any rattles and squeaks the driver hears will have to be eliminated.

Finally, the car is provided with an owner's manual and polished to a high luster.

Building Racing Cars

Soon after the automobile was invented a century or so ago, drivers began racing them. Today, automobile racing is a major sport in the United States, drawing more paying fans than football or baseball.

There are several different types of auto racing. Stock-car racing is No. 1 with most people. In this, cars race on specially built tracks with long straightaways and high-banked turns. Stock cars streak along at speeds of two hundred miles an hour and more, with plenty of "bammin' and jammin'" (banging fenders at high speeds).

While stock cars look like family cars and have familiar names—Ford, Chevrolet, Pontiac, and Buick—they are very different. In building a stock car, the first step is to take apart a production car, that is, an assembly-line car. Then the engine is rebuilt as a racing engine. Special parts—pistons, rods, cams, crankshafts, and carburetors —are added to boost power and speed.

The car's body is rebuilt, too. Steel replaces lighter-weight metal and plastics so the car will be better able to take the stress and strain of racing. In the front-seat area of the car, a boxlike structure of steel tubes is added. Called a roll cage, it prevents the roof from collapsing should the car turn upside down.

Getting a car ready to compete in stock-car competition is expensive. It can cost as much as $60,000 or $70,000.

About one quarter of the cost goes for the engine.

Automobile racing also includes small, low, and very fast Indy cars. Named after the Indianapolis 500, the world's most popular auto race, Indy cars are the fastest racing machines in the world. They can blaze down straightaways at 230 miles an hour. They *average* speeds of 200 miles an hour on oval tracks.

Indy cars are designed something like airplanes. The car's central structure is a tube-shaped shell made of very strong, lightweight material, such as aluminum or carbon fiber. Indy cars are also notable for their front and rear wings. The flow of air over and under the wings produces a "downforce." This presses the car to the track, helping it to go faster on turns.

In building Indy car bodies and engines, there are no assembly lines involved. Parts don't arrive by the truckful. There are no robot workers. Indy cars are manufactured and put together piece by piece, part by part.

British-built cars and British-built engines dominate Indy racing. In fact, at the Indianapolis 500 in 1988, not one American-built car was entered. The most popular chassis is the British March. The easiest way to spot a March is by its high, hoodlike structure, called a cowl, around the driver. The cowl sweeps forward to a sharply pointed nose.

It takes an enormous amount of energy to create an Indy car, and thousands of working hours. And it takes millions of dollars.

Tomorrow's Cars

What are cars of the future going to look like, not the distant future but in the years just ahead?

Cars of tomorrow are going to be sleeker, more rounded in shape. They will be built lower to the ground and will handle easier as a result. Engines will be made mostly of aluminum and they will be more powerful. Some cars will be able to cruise at speeds as high as 150 miles an hour.

There will be more glass in tomorrow's cars, maybe even glass roofs. The driver and passengers will get much more of a feeling of openness. The glass, although thinner than the glass used today, will be stronger.

And cars of the future will offer more electronic controls. For example, when something goes wrong with the car, an electronic monitoring system will be able to tell the mechanic exactly where the trouble is located. Some electronic systems, such as those that control the radio and heater, may be able to respond to the driver's voice commands.

How will cars of the future be fueled? Will battery-powered cars begin to replace those that now burn gasoline? Some experts believe that the practical electric car may be close at hand. Others say that alternative fuels, such as ethanol (a type of alcohol), will see wide use.

But with all of these advances, models will still be made out of clay and engineers will still use computer screens to draw plans for each part. Prototypes will be built and carefully tested. The cars will be ordered into production. And the final stop will still be the dealer's showroom.

Perhaps you may own one of these "cars of the future."

Index

About the Author

George Sullivan is a well-known author of nonfiction books for children, with more than one hundred titles to his credit. He has written on subjects ranging from nuclear submarines to computers and from baseball to photography. Many of Mr. Sullivan's books have received special recognition from such institutions and organizations as the Center for Children's Books, University of Chicago; the Children's Book Committee, Bank Street College; and the New York Public Library.

A graduate of Fordham University, Mr. Sullivan is a member of PEN, the American Society of Journalists and Authors, and the Authors Guild. He lives in New York City with his wife.

About the Artist

Ernie Norcia grew up on a small Connecticut farm where the rural beauty of his surroundings inspired a love of drawing and painting at an early age. After high school, he attended the Rhode Island School of Design, where he earned a Bachelor of Fine Arts degree. He continued his studies at the Maryland Institute College of Art, and graduated with a Master of Fine Arts degree.

His illustrations have appeared in many forms, including national ads, magazines, album covers, and greeting cards. In addition, he has taught at both the high school and university levels. Perhaps the artist's most notable achievement was an Emmy Award for his work on *Cosmos, The Shores of the Cosmic Ocean* by Dr. Carl Sagan, which aired on PBS.

Mr. Norcia has been a member of the Graphic Artists Guild for the past nine years. He lives and works on the outskirts of Dayton, Ohio.

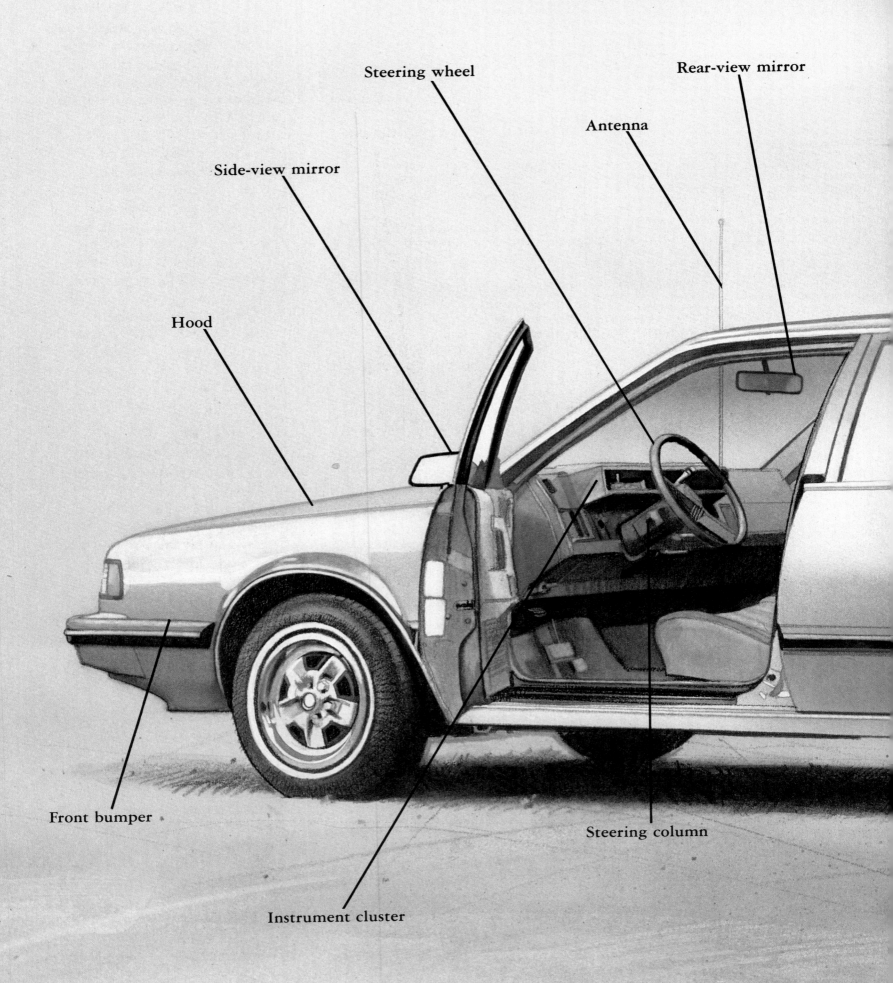

Steering wheel

Rear-view mirror

Antenna

Side-view mirror

Hood

Front bumper

Steering column

Instrument cluster